# WE
## THE PEOPLE
# DE SOTO

Published by Creative Education, Inc. 123 South
Broad Street, Mankato, Minnesota 56001

**Library of Congress Cataloging-in-Publication Data**

Zadra, Dan.
    De Soto : explorer of the Southeast (1500-1542) / Dan Zadra ;
illustrated by Harold Henriksen.

    p. cm. — (We the people)
    Summary: A biography of the wealthy Spanish explorer who became
the first white man to cross the Mississippi.
    ISBN 0-88682-185-1
    1. Soto, Hernando de, ca. 1500-1542—Juvenile literature.
2. Explorers—America—Biography—Juvenile literature.
3. Explorers—Spain—Biography—Juvenile literature.    4. America—
Discovery and exploration—Spanish—Juvenile literature.    [1. De
Soto, Hernando, 1500 (ca.)-1542.    2. Explorers.]    I. Henriksen,
Harold, ill.    II. Title.    III. Series.
E125.S7Z33    1988
970.01'6'0924—dc19
[B]
[92]                                                                87-36383
                                                                       CIP
                                                                        AC

# WE
# *THE PEOPLE*
# DE SOTO

## EXPLORER OF THE SOUTHEAST
## *(1500-1542)*

DAN ZADRA

Illustrated By Harold Henriksen

CREATIVE EDUCATION

# DE SOTO

It was an exciting moment for the young Spaniard. After months at sea, Hernando de Soto tramped down the gangplank of the great sailing ship and stepped out on dry land.

"So this is the New World," he whispered to himself. He was only nineteen, but already a captain's sword jangled from his hip.

Hernando was a conquistador, a cavalry officer—and proud of it. Like thousands of Spaniards before him, he had come to the new land to conquer its Indian people and take their gold. All he owned were his sword

and his armor. But here on the shores
of Central America in the year 1519,
young Captain de Soto said to himself: "I will soon be rich as a king."

De Soto came to the New World
at the time when Cortes was on his

way to conquer Mexico. How he
wished he could have gone with Cortes! Instead, De Soto had to stay in
Panama and serve the Governor.

Hernando was brave and won
favor. Soon, he had filled the

Governor's treasure vaults with gold gathered from Indian raids. "Keep some for yourself," said the Governor. Hernando and a friend used this wealth to build two ships for trading.

Then Hernando heard some exciting news. Francisco Pizarro needed help down in Peru. He was searching for men to help him conquer a kingdom even richer than that of Mexico. The kingdom belonged to the powerful Inca Indians. Legend said that Cuzco, the Inca capital, was layered in fine gold and jewels.

De Soto saw that his chance for great wealth had come! He sailed south with 100 armed men and 50 horses. He met Pizarro on the coast of Ecuador. The two adventurers made a pact together. "Gold or death," they

agreed. De Soto was made second-in-command.

The year was 1532. For eight frustrating years Pizarro had failed to reach the fabled treasure of the Incas. Now, with De Soto's help, he was

about to succeed at last.

The Spanish, 170 strong, road
south across the front range of the
beautiful and mysterious Andes
Mountains.

Ahead lay Caxamarca, where the

Inca emperor, Atahualpa, had his army. Even with armor, muskets and horses, the Spaniards would be no match for the large Inca legions. But De Soto was clever and cunning. He made a plan to lure Atahualpa into a trap.

Pizarro and his handful of conquistadors were waiting. They captured the emperor and held him for ransom. Atahualpa gave them gold worth many millions of dollars. But the Spanish broke their promise and killed him anyway. Hernando de Soto cared little about human life. He returned to Spain in 1536, a rich and famous man.

But wealth was not enough for the greedy conquistador. Hernando wanted power as well. He married

Isabel de Bobadilla, who was the
daughter of Panama's Governor.
Then he asked the King to make him
a governor in the New World.

De Soto was really hoping to be-
come the ruler of Colombia and
Ecuador. But King Charles V of
Spain feared that Pizarro and De Soto
would get together and set up a
powerful empire of their own in
South America.

So he offered De Soto Cuba and

Florida instead, and De Soto accepted. There were rumors that Florida was even richer in gold than Peru—and it was said to hold the legendary Fountain of Youth as well. "Drink from the magic fountain and eternal youth will be yours," went the legend.

In 1538, Hernando de Soto, his wife, and a well-equipped army set sail from Spain. They had 237 horses, some fighting dogs, livestock, and a rich assortment of trade goods.

When he arrived in Havana, he set up his wife as governor. He sent some ships to scout the coast of Florida and find a good landing place. It was his intention to explore and seize all the lands of the Gulf Coast.

On May 30, 1539, he landed at

Tampa Bay. Once again, De Soto's stern brown eyes glistened with greed as he gazed across the Florida landscape. He swaggered to his horse, mounted up and signalled his army forward. There were 1,000 soldiers, and a huge herd of pigs would serve as food along the way. De Soto planned to capture Indians as guides. But a great stroke of luck made this unnecessary.

An army patrol found a Spaniard, Juan Ortiz, living with the Indians. Ortiz had come to Florida ten years before, with another expedition. He was captured and had lived with the Indians ever since.

Ortiz became De Soto's guide and helped make peace with the local Indians. The Indian chief told De

Soto: "There is no gold in this country. Gold is found in the North." So the Spanish army moved forward into the wilderness. Now De Soto's luck ran out. Day after day, his armored men slogged through eerie swamps and across wide rivers. They caught malaria from the mosquitos. Huge leeches clung to their skin. Poisonous snakes slid silently through the dark water. Indians lay in ambush to shoot them with armor-piercing arrows. But still the Spaniards pressed on.

Near the Suwannee River, De Soto's men had a battle with 400 Indian warriors. This time they fought in the open and the Spaniards won. Again, they pressed on northward, still searching vainly for gold.

News of the invasion flew ahead
of them. The Indians heard that
demon warriors with hairy faces and
fiery weapons were coming. The

people fled in panic from their villages, leaving behind the food they had harvested. De Soto spent the winter in northern Florida. His fleet came up from Tampa with supplies.

The next spring, De Soto heard about an Indian queen who lived toward the east. It was said she had gold! The army marched into Georgia. They found the queen—but her "gold" was only copper.

Disappointed, they pressed on into South Carolina. Then they turned northwest and probably passed through part of North Carolina and Tennessee. Then they went southward again, into Alabama.

The long adventure was taking a fierce toll on De Soto's men. Fighting, sickness and death were constant companions. Some soldiers deserted the army and went off to live with friendly tribes. In Fall, 1540, De Soto entered the land of the proud and powerful Choctaw tribe.

These fierce Indians decided to stop the invaders, once and for all. At a large Indian city named Movilla, De Soto and his army were trapped. They fought savagely against overwhelming numbers of Indians. Finally, by setting the town on fire, the Spaniards won. But they had lost many of their men and almost all of their equipment.

Now De Soto's men begged him to march to the coast, to go home. It was good advice, but De Soto's mind

was clouded by the worst type of fever—*gold fever.*

They pushed on through the winter, travelling northwest, growing more and more ragged with each mile. Then on May 8, 1541, they came to the bank of an immense river. De Soto sat spellbound in the

saddle. Finally, he said: "We will call it Rio Grande." It was the Mississippi.

The mighty river was two miles wide, but De Soto insisted they must cross it. They built barges. A fleet of "canoe Indians" came to investigate, but the army was able to drive them away.

De Soto now led his dwindling force into Arkansas. Wherever he went, he asked about gold. But the Indians always told him it was to be found farther on.

So they kept marching.

In the spring of 1542, De Soto decided to return to the sea. Only about 300 men and 40 horses were left. His guide, Juan Ortiz, had died. They came again to the banks of the mighty river, the Mississippi. And

there Hernando de Soto fell ill—perhaps of malaria, perhaps of fatigue
and disappointment. He died on May
21, 1542.

His men, fearful that the Indians
would dig up his body, buried him in
the river he had discovered.

Then the remnant of the

conquistador's army went southwest into the parched Texas badlands. They hoped to reach Mexico. But they were stopped by deserts and turned back to the river.

In December, 1542, they reached the Mississippi again. There they built crude ships to take them downstream.

On September 10, 1543, they reached a Spanish settlement in Mexico. Of the original army, only 311 men returned alive. Their leader was dead, and there was no gold to line their pockets. Humbled, many of the men sank silently to their knees and prayed.

# WE THE PEOPLE SERIES

## WOMEN OF AMERICA

CLARA BARTON
JANE ADDAMS
ELIZABETH BLACKWELL
HARRIET TUBMAN
SUSAN B. ANTHONY
DOLLEY MADISON

## INDIANS OF AMERICA

GERONIMO
CRAZY HORSE
CHIEF JOSEPH
PONTIAC
SQUANTO
OSCEOLA

## FRONTIERSMEN OF AMERICA

DANIEL BOONE
BUFFALO BILL
JIM BRIDGER
FRANCIS MARION
DAVY CROCKETT
KIT CARSON

## WAR HEROES OF AMERICA

JOHN PAUL JONES
PAUL REVERE
ROBERT E. LEE
ULYSSES S. GRANT
SAM HOUSTON
LAFAYETTE

## EXPLORERS OF AMERICA

COLUMBUS
LEIF ERICSON
DeSOTO
LEWIS AND CLARK
CHAMPLAIN
CORONADO